Existentialism:
The Musical

Derek Zanetti

illustrations by Seth LeDonne

to lindsey, my partner in crime
(also my first wife)

Special thanks to Seth Ledonne, Matt Ussia,
Joe Mruk, Mike Miller, Hiedi Niebauer, and
Tom Cox — you guys helped me out a ton
when I felt like giving up.

introduction

Hello newfound friend, I'm glad we are finally able to meet. I never thought it would ever happen this way, but I sure am glad that it finally did happen. It has taken me all of thirty years to prepare these stories to show you, that I once existed in a different way than I do now. I have a hard time remembering the past as it actually happened, but every once in a while, I'm able to grab a glimpse of clarity and write a few moments of truth down.

I always said that I wanted to write a book about my feelings to see if anyone feels the same way that I do. I often wondered if I shared the same thoughts as a complete stranger from all the way across the globe and never knew about it. I thought to myself, how will anyone ever know if they are the only one that feels the way that they feel, if no one ever shares anything about their feelings? Maybe you aren't all alone in the thoughts you have, and maybe I'm not all alone either? Or maybe we can be all alone together?

We all have demons that we have to wrestle. We all have doubts and fears and insecurities. Anyone who says otherwise is just a salesman, trying to seem superior to the whole thing. I never planned on defeating or conquering any of my demons. I just thought that wrestling with them was a good way to start feeling better about the giant nothing that hangs over our heads.

Well I hope you like it.

preface: two letters

Hey man,

    I don't mean to bum you out, but I just want to say this before I explode.

    Every day is the same old thing. Wake up, get showered, get dressed, go to work, come home exhausted, eat, drink, and sleep. And every once in a while, something else will happen, like going to church, or to a baseball game, or a funeral. I don't like what I do for a living; yet still everyday I do it. Casual Friday is nice, and I get 2 Mondays off a month. My bank account grows until I buy something new that I've always wanted, but soon or later the new thing I bought is just another old thing I have, that I don't care about anymore. I shine my shoes just for them to get dirty and scuffed again. My office building feels like a mass grave. It doesn't have a smell. The fbrescent lights buzz in my mind hours after I come home. I'm supposed to be getting a raise at the end of the month, but even with that as the great motivator, it doesn't make any difference. I still want to die most of the time.

    Anyway I hope you're well, Kevin

Hey Dude,

Thanks for writing back so quickly.

Coffee, cigarettes, organic vegan wrap, read a book, walk, drinks, cigarettes, sometimes sex. I thought punk rock was supposed to make me feel alive. I feel like I'm in a goddamn Twilight Zone episode, or Groundhog's Day or something like that. I always said I never was going to grow up, that the system of rules, and boundaries, and regulation that all these morons put themselves through is everything that is wrong with America. But what the hell am I doing? I mean yeah, it's cool to not be a slave to some corporate dead end job, but I feel like I'm at the dead end of something else. It's so isolating, so cold. I feel like a prisoner to a jail I've made for my self, and I walk around with my torment as a badge of honor. I used to look at all the suits walking to and from work, and I would pity them. I would say how awful it must be to be them, but more and more, I think... man, I would trade them places any day. I must have really fucked up.

Well I guess that's me in a nutshell, Matt

the first question i asked myself before unplugging

I bet this isn't any kind of breaking NEWS to you,
but you are one day going to die.
Maybe today,
Maybe in 80 years.
Who really knows?
What if today was it?
What if today was your last day here?
Would you look back and say you did what YOU wanted?
Would you be content with how it all worked out?
Did you go everywhere you wanted to go?
Did you see everything you wanted to see?
Did you spend too much time in worry to really enjoy
anything?
Did you smile enough?
Did you laugh enough?
Did you let other people tell you what was best for you?
Have you been afraid to be yourself?
Did people know how you really felt?
You can't change the past,
it's far too late for that.
And there is no certainty of any kind of future.
You do however for sure have right now to be alive.
So live, or one day you may grow to regret it.

the certainty of going to church

These old church buildings that used to be something are making me feel like a tax return I'll never get. Like a garbage can filled with unread gospel tracts. Like an empty prayer, followed by an empty communion wine cup. Like being a Gentile, before it was OK to be a Gentile. Everyone's got this feeling that they are doing the right thing while they are doing it, until years later they look back at what they where doing and think, "What the hell was I thinking? "

Its OK to be wrong . . . everybody. It's not wrong to be wrong, it's just wrong to think that you never can be. It's living with this unshakable certainty that your answers are the best answers and that everyone else who has answers that are different that yours is wrong. That is what makes hindsight so painful. That is what makes the church pew so uncomfortable for me. It's the certainty of being certain, while never being able to admit that you are scared of being wrong.

And I have been scared. Scared of God. Scared of Hell. Scared of women. Scared that women will send me to Hell. Scared of failure. Failure is the greatest gift God has ever given to us. It's the best way for us to know that God is God, and we are not. Failure is a gift for anyone who wants to feel like it's OK to just be yourself.

a church story

There I was , like I just awoke from a coma, standing in line in the middle of a church building somewhere in Ohio, very afraid. The man at the pulpit was yelling the word sin. He was going on about abortion, homosexuality, and masturbation. I was 15.

The most awful music was playing in the background. It sounded like a strong mix of U2, Mumford and Sons, and guilt. The kids were dressed like kids. The adults tried to look younger than they were, which made me uneasy. I was obviously out of place.

There was a man pushing people over by their foreheads. They lay on the ground lifeless. Some were crying, some were speaking in strange tongues. I just stood there in a line feeling out of sorts. I felt naked, like I was in a public shower, being filmed for a snuff film. However I continued to stand in line, for fear of being different.

I didn't want to go to Hell. I didn't want to make God angry. I didn't want to feel naked and ashamed. I didn't know what else to do. The yelling preacher put his hands on my 15 year old forehead. I didn't feel anything. He kept it there. He prayed louder and faster. More people gathered around me. I felt like I was naked, I felt like I was being led to the slaughter. I was filled with anxiety, I was filled with doubt, I didn't feel God, or love, I didn't feel forgiven. I didn't feel anything. My only defense was to fall over. So I did. The people cheered. I've lain there lifeless and confused ever since.

documentaries about going to hell

The clouds began to spit lightly a mist over the cars and street. The sun went hiding from us here in Pittsburgh. The air tasted grey. And everything looked as if it were dirty. Some popular rap song was playing from the trunk of a car that was now filling with the rain now coming at the earth a bit harder, a bit larger, and growing in momentum. I could smell copper. The light company was working on the power lines down the street in the rain . . . That can't be safe.

After being alive for so long you start to think that maybe the world isn't going to end after all. That maybe there has already been a number of apocalyptic times already, and the people who died, died in the apocalypse, and the people who survived, got to live. I can remember as a young person being very uneasy about the Rapture. Hearing the trumpets sound, the dead rising from their graves, and all of the faithful saints being tractor-beamed into the clouds. I can remember wondering if I would make the cut, if my sins where forgivable (as a 12 year old). I wondered if I would ever see my friends and family again. Church was a weekly reminder of my sin and a constant companion to the anxiety of missing the Rapture.

I can remember hearing that if my parents didn't homeschool me, that means they didn't love me, that my soul was in jeopardy of contamination if I kept secular company. I was told that the music I liked to listen to had demonic voices subliminally layered into it to try and get me to do evil things. That God was an angry jealous God who would smite the sinners that needed smiting, but yet loved us so much that he made a way to keep us from hell. I can remember wanting to know what I needed to do to be counted in that number, when the saints go marching in, and if I could somehow sneak in a copy of Weezer's *Pinkerton* on cassette tape through the pearly gates.

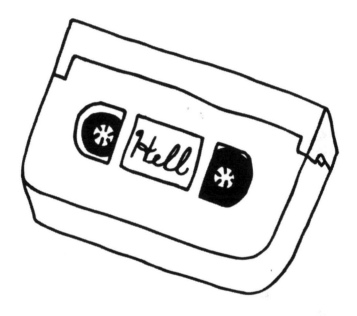

I want to be SAVED

These church marquees are trying to say what's best for me
Like everyone in this country doesn't know they exist
Or what they have to say
Like they are offering something new
In their debt ridden offering plates

I feel like my senses are under assault
I feel belittled
Like a billboard
Like a beer commercial
Like masturbating with sandpaper
Like a megaphone in the eardrum of my mind

Some snarky smart-ass catch phrase
to make you want to be on their side of the joke
Like some secret handshaking club
Like being led to the gas chamber
Like being taken to the judge for sentencing
On your knees begging for forgiveness

The church marquees usually say something like this:
Something something something...blood of Christ
Blah blah blah...burning in hell for eternity
How is it supposed to make me feel?
Guilty, thankful?
It certainly isn't making me want to come into your dead
sanctuary

Or be a part of your dead dances
Or believe in your dead American plastic fast food god
Or buy your dead brainwashed feel good prosperity BMW
gated community gospel

Maybe there is a reason why your buildings are empty even
when they are full

Dear Jesus,
Help my unbelief
Forgive me
If that's still a thing

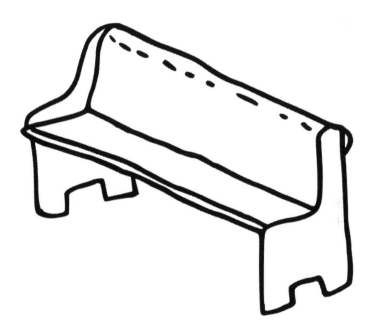

one way train ride

On a train, headed east to Johnstown, Pennsylvania. It is rainy and cold. Kind of like the rainy and cold you don't expect in the middle of August, but the kind of rainy and cold you come to know when you've lived in Pittsburgh all your life. It's odd to see the town and the houses from this view.

Along the tracks and under the bridges are mountains of trash left by the traveling punk kids with the dogs and face tattoos. It's very green out there, past the graffiti, and the crumbling wall that it sits on. Coal draggers pass by on either side with great speed, taking fuel from mill to mill. There are a lot of old abandoned buildings along the tracks, which makes me feel good. I kind of know how they feel.

There is a reservoir filled with chocolate milk, and a mixture of plastic and Styrofoam outside of an old factory that has been seemingly forgotten. The rails are bumpy, as the train car sways back and forth as we travel across. Sometimes you can find a great peace inside of abandonment. Sometimes a dead end is the best thing that can happen to you. Sometimes there is great solace in the abandoned buildings, and homes, and factories. There are no billboards on this path, no McDonald's, nothing making you feel bad about just sitting and being yourself. Aside from the vibrations of the train, and the fan blowing from the door behind the coach car, the ride had a peaceful quiet hum to it. It's soothing and reminds me of what I always thought the voice of God might sound like, gentle but not perfect.

To the left of the rails heading east-bound you can see a junkyard the size of 100 football fields, filled with cars, buses and what seems to be an entire fleet of tow trucks. I never really thought about it until now I guess, but who tows the tow truck, when the tow truck needs a tow? I had never seen so many like that just sitting there, forgotten about. I guess even doctors need a doctor from time to time; I've just never seen a bunch of sick doctors sitting in a doctor's office. But then again, I don't spend much time in waiting rooms, like that.

I think traveling has been, in a way a kind of medicine for me. Some kind of magical potion that has allowed me to be okay with not feeling normal. It's a great reminder that there are people and things that exist outside of my little world. People to meet, things to just look at with new eyes, and brand new feelings to feel that you never knew you had, living inside of you. There is so much to see and do just outside your very own window.

my therapist session

The Doctor says to me, "If what they say is true, then all you need is a mustard-sized piece, and you, my friend, have it. It's more than what I have anyway, I wish I had even a mustard-sized piece, but I don't have shit. Hold on to that, man; don't let anyone take it from you.

"There's so much bullshit to distract you from what is right in front of you. The news, the paper, the war, the drugs, the medication, the pressure to be a man, the pressure to succeed, buy a home, make a family, look like you are effortlessly holding it all together. What is success, and who is successful? The president? Bernie Madoff? Donald Trump? What kind of life is that? Surely they have money and people know who they are, but what the hell is it all for?? You have something that they can never have, innocence . . . a mustard seed. Innocence is the one of the only things you can't get back once its gone, other than time, and your virginity. You have to protect your mustard seed, for Christ's sake you got to protect it. The fact that you have a mustard seed gives me hope that maybe it's not to late for me to have a mustard seed of my own someday. It gives me hope for my children, that maybe they can have a mustard seed.

"Who said that being impressive was all that great? All these people get all this money and fame. Shit, and then what? They get noticed for being a morbidly average puppet, and then one day lose their mind cause they realize that they aren't everything that everyone expected of them. Look at all the time people spend watching these people, admiring them, worshipping them, dressing like them, talking like them, and following them. The next time you feel like killing yourself, first thing call me, if I don't answer, take out your mustard seed, and keep calling me until I answer."

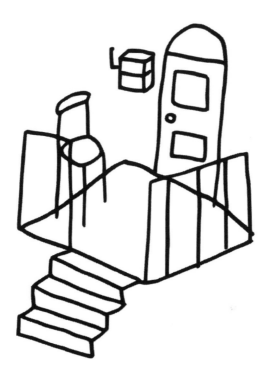

clinical depression

I was too drunk to feel anything; I guess that's where I wanted to be. My eyes where swimming in my head. Grease had covered my face. My mouth was dry, my head spinning like a top. My hands shaking, my memory poor, and my ability to tell the truth was worse that usual. I even smoked a fair amount of someone else's cigarettes. My fingers smelled bad. My eyes burned and were itchy.

I had worked enough to know that it was just a distraction. It kept me busy enough to just forget that there where more important things to do than just keep my head above water. Who determined how deep the water is supposed to be anyway, and what, if not everyone, is able to keep afloat in the same way as everyone else? Who made these rules? I just want to do what I want to do. And sometimes that's nothing. Is that such a horrible thing?

Maybe I'll get a job at the Salvation Army, that seems like something I wouldn't hate too bad, as long as I didn't have to be there all the time. Maybe if I can just go in like 2 days a week, just enough to give money to the people who need it from me. And the rest of the time, I can just think about things or play my guitar or the record player. Maybe Ill just wake up one day and walk along the railroad tracks as far as I can go and turn around and come back home. And maybe that's what I can do with the time that I have. Does that make me crazy? It's no less crazy spending the whole day in an office doing things that don't mean anything to get money that means even less. For some people, the idea of a career in some field of work is a great way to feel accomplished or successful, but not everyone feels that way.

Is that wrong?

Is that so wrong to feel different, to feel lost all the time? I thought long and hard about what it might look like to be some sort of politician, but suicide is not an option at this point. I want to help people in some way, even if I can just be a good buddy or a reliable pen pal.

Most people don't know how to react when you tell them you struggle with depression. Some people just say get over it. I had one old friend ask if I was oversensitive or just gay. I'm just trying my best to not hate myself. Today. I guess I'm doing ok.

money: a race to nothing

Like knowing I'm going die from diabetes,
in a doughnut factory.
Like how I feel when they pass the basket in church.
Like the weeks and months that have been lost
toiling in some room for a base hourly wage
doing something you hate,
yet having to return to it
because you believe in some weird twisted way
that you can't have life with out it.
Kind of like letting your husband beat you
when he's mad and drunk,
but loving him anyway because divorce is a sin.
An empty pack of cigarettes at the end of the day
sending you back to the job that you hate.
A whole pile of brand new clothes
that you wear just to impress people who will never learn your
name.
Like a fake tan faded.
Like the toilet in a Golden Corral restaurant
on Father's Day
in San Antonio, Texas
with no air conditioning and no toilet paper.

I've grown to be so worried,
so nervous over this debt we all carry.
This imaginary greed that's supposed to make me feel secure.
These weights and measures that keep us bound.

Looking more attractive
having nicer things
being envied
the talk of the town.
Having things worth stealing and being willing to kill
to protect it.

Work harder to waste more
On vacation in the middle of some Wal-Mart cruse ship
with free margaritas and cheese dip
Broken designer sunglasses
left feeling empty
in a big empty house
with a fake empty smile.
No real friends
No time to think
No time to be free.
Always afraid of losing what people think of you.

Some goddamned altar call at a youth group tent revival
meeting where people repent and beg for salvation to a god
that only exists in the fearmongering of some old-tired rhetoric
used to keep people in some safe little trap or a chain smoker
hoping to be a hand model.

Like how nobody cares about Milli Vanilli,
or Kevin Federline anymore…
or the bigger question,
did anyone in the first place?

I got things to do

I don't have time for suicide notes,
or riverside gambling boats,
or sore throats.
And I ain't going to vote for the next political leader,
or pay a palm reader,
give in to paying some parking meter.
I surely don't have time to get myself caught in my zipper.

I got things to do, man. Big things to do.
Like hug my mom, and tell her I love her.
Like helping the old lady down the street take out her trash.
Like pretending to stay awake at church, for my soul's sake.
Like recycle.
Like forgiving myself every day.

Like trying with every breath to remain present.
Trying to not buy so much shit that I'll never use.
To be thankful.
I don't have time to be sad anymore,
to slam my front door,
and cry on my front porch

I don't have time to watch FOX News,
give myself the blues,
or worry about the Apocalypse.

I don't have time for talent search TV,
or reality TV,
and I certainly don't have time for no MTV.
I got things to do, my friend.
Big things to do.

Like be a good friend.
Like write a nice birthday card.
Like visit someone's grandma who doesn't have any visitors.
Like smile.

I got things to do, Dad. Big things to do.
Like rake all the leaves,
in my backyard,
into a pile,
and jump into them,
forever.

I want to cry

I want to cry, I mean honestly, I really want to cry.
And not like one tear of sadness or loneliness, but like buckets of bitter tears.
The kind of tears you fill an aquarium with.
Like getting picked on in gym class tears.
Like the tears you shed when you deliver phone books for a living.
I want my lungs to shake.
I want my bottom lip to quiver.
I want to soak the collar of my shirt.
I want to feel my spirit leave my body and return with more tears.
I want to put myself to sleep I cry so hard.
I've thought of every sad thought I could possibly think
and I can't for the life of me
let go and just cry.
Maybe something is wrong with me.

a story from being honest

The ghost inside of me came out and became my best friend the day I decided not to have any more secrets. Most of the time I'm scared of how everything is going to turn out because of all the bad seeds I've sewn in other people's gardens. For all the upside-down flags I've flown, for pissing in the water fountains of my past, I'm afraid.

It took me longer than I thought to become honest with myself, but once I was able to do that, being honest with everyone else was easier than anything else could be. In my dreams I remember swimming in the hallways of my elementary school over the heard of my unaware class mates, using some rudimentary doggy paddle or freestyle stroke to get to places I took for granted.

The secrets I used to shield myself from became the very fears that placed me in the paralyzing coma that I just now came out of. Now be sure to know that in my coma I was very much aware of everything going on around me, I was even aware of the ghost that was living inside of me.

However. I did not yet know of its purpose.

This story will continue.

johnston ave

It had been raining since well before I was awake, and it didn't look like it would be stopping any time soon. The sky was a fast-food-burger-patty grey, and I could see Noah's Arc floating past my house on a raft of Styrofoam, and disposable diapers from up the hill where the Section 8 housing was. My neighbor, who has black teeth, was chain-smoking menthol cigarettes in her bathing suit praying that she still had more minutes on her TracFone so that she can call the candy man.

Sometimes you wake up in the morning and all you want is a ray of sunshine, something to remind you that last night is in the past and today is a brand new chance to be whoever you want to be.

Sometimes there is no such thing as second chances.

Sometimes Jesus is on the other train, heading in a different direction.

Sometimes your mother dies of cancer, and the first thing you do is pick up a cigarette habit.

It's hard to feel forgiven when all you do is think about how you could have been different in the past. And it's real hard too see a brighter future when the words "DEAD END" are written in jet-black letters on the inside of your eyelids. It's nice to try to pretend away what you've done, especially when all it does is rain inside your mind.

-A letter I wrote to myself in my dreams-

a pen pal in the digital age

I've been thinking a lot lately about gathering a few pen pals from all over the place to write to. I think it would be nice to have a few jokes to tell someone in a letter. I can imagine them laughing quietly to themselves. I think would be nice to come home after being away for a while with a stack of letters awaiting my attention, like a trusty dog, but without all the messy clean up. Something to devote some time to, something to collect over time.

I want to start carrying a pen and leather bound book around. I like how it makes me feel when I buy a book of stamps, especially when I don't know where they will go. I think about waking up early, making a pot of strong coffee, my pen and paper on my dining room table while I share my secrets with the person on the other end of a letter. I think about how warm the mailbox will feel knowing that there is something inside of it other than a light bill or some ugly supermarket advertisement. I think about how the mailman must feel, knowing that he is bringing a new adventure to someone's otherwise boring life. Maybe that someone will be me.

Maybe writing letters to a pen pal would help me become better at telling the truth. Maybe it will help me be honest with myself. And maybe if I try really hard I can even draw a doodle or picture in one of the corners. Sometimes life feels like waiting in a car in a parking lot filled with oil-stained parking spaces. Maybe getting a letter in the mail would fix that. I have been growing very bored with getting my information and correspondence from the information super highway. It's lonely out there. I wish I could experience more intimate ways of hearing from people, and what their lives are about.

It's not always good to keep it all to yourself. It's not healthy to not to share things with others. I really look forward to writing a tune I can whistle as I walk to the mailbox...maybe we can write it together, in a letter.

351 Johnston Ave. Pittsburgh, PA 15207

someone else's shoes

There are whole piles of shoes
my foot will never fit into
Some shoes are too small
too narrow
or just don't fit right
And I don't have the time
to try to walk around in shoes that don't fit
I barely have time to do what I need to do
in the shoes I was given
It's important to see the world
through someone else's perspective
But your feet can only take you
to so many places
In someone else's shoes

guilty dream

There's this big wooden door just behind my eyes that creaks and cracks every time it's either opened or closed. The knob is rusty. It turns your palms orange. Sometimes there's an old version of Bob Dylan smoking Lucky Strike cigarettes, wearing a leopard-skin pill-box hat, just days before that day he is supposed to die, on a rocking chair, telling me that this whole thing is a joke. The snaps and pops of an old 78 record are fresh in the air. I can see a ceiling fan is on in the hallway, but it doesn't make a sound. There is always a cat on the banister at the bottom of the stairwell. I hate cats. It tastes like black coffee in my mouth. I don't mind that all that much.

In the faint distance, like the low hum of a harmonica tuned to F sharp, I can hear my middle sister being happy. Laughing, enjoying the time she is given as a child laughing, pretending, and enjoying the freedom of her imagination. This memory makes me sad, because I'm not sure she feels that way all that much any more. I think maybe it was hard for her sometimes to feel ok with the skin she was given. Maybe I did a bad job of protecting her feelings, as her older brother. Maybe I was more of a bully than her caretaker. Maybe I could have been more kind, a little more gentle. Maybe things would be different.

I usually wake up shortly after I hear her laughing, and playing to herself and have to wash my face with the holy water I keep in a bucket under my steps in the basement. Sometimes, I make it back to bed after that, most times I just lay on the couch until the sun rises, trying not to repeat my bad behaviors. Trying to wear a kinder face, a more gentle coat, trying to be different. Now, I have regret.

Milk Crates

So, I've been stealing these milk crates from the Dairy Mart down the street to store my junk in. I guess don't really consider it stealing, because if they were a valued item, the Dairy Mart would do a better job of keeping them away from the unmarked dumpster on the side of the road. I only take the black ones; I neatly stack the rest in a nicer pile than how I found them, in square box shape behind the unmarked dumpster.

One night, I went back there at around 11 p.m., and there was a homeless man sleeping behind the dumpster. He was passed out drunk and smelled like sour milk. Even with all the commotion I made shuffling through the piles of milk crates, he didn't lose a wink of sleep. For a moment there I wondered if maybe he was dead, because I made a loud crash when I moved a stack of orange milk crates, but I noticed his snow-white belly moving up and down and his gin-blossomed nose flaring in and out. So, I knew he was just a heavy sleeper, or really drunk, or deaf.

Either way, it wasn't any of my business. I just wanted to grab a dozen or so milk crates and get home. Besides, I have a hard time feeling bad for white people who are homeless. It's probably just my perception, but I also happen to be white, and someone who came from odd circumstances of my very own, and I seem to be doing all right. At least all right enough to not be sleeping behind the unmarked dumpster in the dairy mart parking lot and smelling like sour milk. But I guess that's even still better than some?

Anyhow, I've been taking all the extra crates that I don't use and making shelving units out of them by zip tying them together and lining the shelves with old cardboard, and shelving paper. I then take them to the flea market where all the hipsters shop and sell them for 30$. I realize that I may not change the world, or whatever, but every Saturday I sell about 5 shelves and I haven't had to take a real job now in over 18 months. So yeah . . . thanks Dairy Mart.

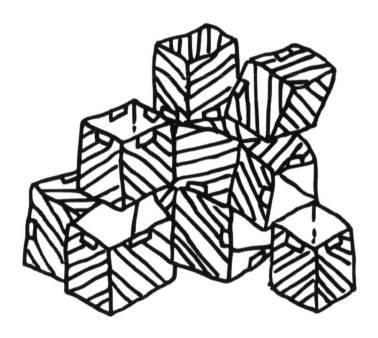

the Ivandale hoarder

There's a crack down the back of my backyard sidewalk
There's a van filled with cans that no one talks about
There is siding that's hiding on the shy side up north
My one neighbor is a hoarder, who sleeps on her porch

She burns plastic bags in an old oil drum
She collects Mary statues; she even offered me one
But I am no Catholic; so I had to refuse,
But I'm sure she's hording something that we all could use

There's a line filled with sheets, drying in the wind
The tin cans are overflowing in the recycling bin.
She has an old tire swing that sways back and forth
My one neighbor is a hoarder, who sleeps on her porch

The magic of the traffic and the bright lights at night
Keeps the cars driving far and the gas prices high
And the bags full of shit that my neighbor re gifts
Are great around Christmas, but makes her house smell like
piss

Her husband divorced her, in June '93
So she bought up three houses at the end of the street,
Now they're full of old groceries, and bags from the junk store
She moved back with her ex husband, who now too sleeps on
the porch

He acquired lung cancer, and breathes with a tank
His hair mostly gray, his ex wife is to thank.
He sits on a chair while he wheezes and hacks
He prays Jesus help me please, but he never hears back

She has a red van that is filled to the top
Of old shoes, baseball cards, and a janitors mop
She has no idea what she's saving it for
My one neighbor is a hoarder, who sleeps on her porch

sleep over conversation

I'm really interested in having a sleep over with all my friends that talk in their sleep, so I can record it and make an avant-garde indie record. Like the really odd Bjork stuff mixed in a blender with a gold fish speaking Russian backwards, but less eerie. Sometimes, I wish I could be weird like that; so that all my alone time did not seem so wasteful. Weird people are supposed to be lonely, that's why they create such awesome weird shit, but if you're not weird, being lonely is just this huge waste of time. Being weird only pays off for like .05% of all weird people.

The rest of them just ride the bus, reading books out of the dollar section, in sweatpants, eating a whole stick of pepperoni while wearing winter mittens, a week after memorial day. Their bald spots look painful, their teeth yellow in a way that reminds me of a manila folder from the free clinic, most of them are fat, they sometimes wear a fanny pack, and not the cool kind that they sell at Urban Outfitters, like the ones you send away for with 850 points from Betty Crocker box tops. White high tops, grass stains. The weird women usually have bangs of some sort. And well more than half of them either believe in unicorns, or Jesus, or in some cases both. And they love to put bumper stickers on things that aren't bumpers.

I hope to get to meet some of these wonderful of people; I hope they some day want to be my friend. I very much want them to come over my house for dinner, on a random Tuesday night for a potluck. I'm so interested in what they would bring and how they would present it. Whether it would be in a pot, or a casserole dish, maybe it would just be an old can of corn, or cocktail wieners.

I certainly don't want to talk about punk rock or tattoos. I don't want to talk about collecting vinyl or politics. I don't want to bring up any topics that I usually go to, that bring me comfort and safety.

I just want to fully sit there and be present, and give to them my attention, and ask real questions about their lives. I want to be interested in what they have to say. I want to watch the way they chew their food or talk with their mouth full. I want to hear the patterns in their laughter.

I want them to make a regular Tuesday night potluck. I want them to bring their one friend over. I then want to befriend that person. I want to build a friendship. I want to have a potluck dinner at my house every Tuesday night for a solid 2 years with all the most different people I can find, people who don't have a lot of friends, people who will share their secrets with me. I want to watch the way they chew their food. I want to ask them questions about their lives, their jobs, their cats. I want to know if they talk in their sleep. And then, I want to invite them over for a sleep over and record it.

Sometimes, I wish someone would invite me to their house for a random Tuesday night potluck.

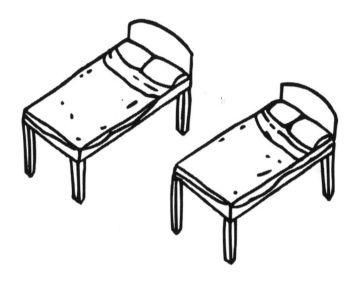

expensive shoes

Sometimes when I'm sitting in my favorite seat at my favorite coffee shop, either to read or to write, or catch up with a friend, the jerks from American Eagle Outfitters headquarters will parade in with their loud voices, texting, and flailing about in a most annoying way.

At what point in time do you decide that you want to be one of these dingus burgers? I thought to myself, as I looked darkly into my white chocolate mocha. One day, I saw them whispering to themselves and pointing at my friend's shoes. Now, as far as I can tell, they were just plain old average leather shoes, nothing special, nothing grand, but for some reason they were captivated by these old brown shoes. One of them broke off of the crowd and asked where she had gotten those shoes. She replied that they were bought at the Antique Boutique from her Aunt Debbie who lives in Indiana, and she wasn't sure of anything about them. My friend bore the same depth of distain for the corporate fashionistas that I had, so was reluctant to offer any assistance. Another girl had broken out of line and joined her fellow co- worker and began to ogle over these shoes. They spent the better part of five minutes lavishly smothering my friend with complements in an effort to break her down and get her to open up a bit about the shoes. The girl finally asked if she could photograph the shoes for research. My friend sharply declined and said she was feeling uncomfortable. They apologized and went about their business.

Upon leaving ,they approached us one last time and said something I'll never forget for the rest of my life. They gently and quietly crouched down to be at eye level with her and offered my friend $200 for the shoes she was wearing. I looked wide-eyed at the table with no words to even say. Before I could look up, my friend's shoes were off and on the table, and the guy put two hundred dollar bills next to her coffee mug, took the shoes, and walked out. I was absolutely speechless.

We silently gathered our belongings, laptops, books, to go coffee mugs. and exited through the back. We walked down the ramp and headed to the Goodwill that shared an adjacent parking lot. Where I assumed we where going to hunt for a new pair of shoes, so my friend wouldn't have to go barefoot through the Southside. When we walked through the doors, she led me to a table full of the same shoes she has just sold. There had to have been 30 pairs of the same identical shoes marked at $3.99. She looked at me and smiled and said, "I don't have an aunt Debbie." I smiled back; she bought the shoes and then took me out for a fancy lunch in one of those fancy upscale outdoor diners.

high school doomsday preppers

I'm not sure what changed for me since the day high school was over, but I surely don't think the same way as I once did. I guess at the time, I wanted the same things that most middle class kids wanted: college, a decent job, friends to drink beer with on the weekends, perhaps I'd even find salvation. But somewhere in between the day I signed those college papers and the day I got my first job with credentials, I realized something about the frailty of life. It's short. I mean it's really short, and there's a whole pile of things I want to see and do before I'm too old to go out and get after it.

Maybe it was that 9/11 thing, or maybe a few years later when my best friend died suddenly in a motorcycle accident, but I did realize that I was going to die, and it would be a real shame if I just sat back and waited for something or somebody to hand me opportunity, or the means to go out into the world and live.

I already had ideas about the system, the way the world works, the way you got to keep working hard to earn money to spend that money on things that break so you can just buy them again in some frail hope to keep the economy going. I knew that politicians weren't magical people. I knew that cops where just bullies with guns. I knew war was just an agreement between two or three rich people to strike fear in the hearts of everyone else. I knew that the poor folks need war as a hope to get out or their poverty, and war needed the poor to die. I had a pretty good idea that there was a God somewhere, but I wasn't convinced one way or another.

The idea of Jesus was cool, savior or not, the idea that rebellion can save the human race was so cool to me. I was pretty sure that most of his followers were just investment bankers in disguise. So I never really wanted to associate myself with any of them. I guess it took me a bit longer to realize that.

The one thing I realized about everything I had questioned is that everything, everything, everything revolves around this thing called money. War, college, church, feeling normal, all cost money. High school prepared you for college, college prepared you for life, and life is this long trail of car buying, war mongering, voting, house buying, wedding planning, buying a new toaster, brakes on your car so you can drive it to the job you need to have in order to pay for the brake pads that wear out. A bigger house, newer car, better job, better pay, more hours, better toaster...finally able, you pay off those collage loans, now you have more money to do things. Maybe you get a habit? Maybe you pick up cigarettes.

And sure, they give you a vacation in the summer, where you spend a month's worth of income to run yourself ragged doing a bunch of "fun" things just so you can take a picture of it to remind you that you have something to look forward to all year, that is better that the other 50 weeks a year you spend hating everything .

Christmas always reminds you to polish up the toaster, and that you have family to impress, and the third Thursday in November tells you to be thankful for your family, and soldiers, and freedom, and toasters. But doesn't it all just seem like a few well-timed out distractions from the need to feel like you have to use the best years of your life to produce grease for this big machine.

Now, even with all of that in the forefront of my brain, knowing that it's all a big curtain, a smoke screen, one big joke, I still am in some ways very much a part of it. Unless you want to be some recluse in a rusted out old bus in the middle of nowhere, you have to participate in some way. But how that applies to me, I have no idea. I mean I'm married. I own a house. I have boxes of records and a whole drawer of different colored underwear. I love boxed wine and leftover pizza. I buy seeds for my garden. I buy tobacco for my pipe. I buy books for my mind, and I buy things for my wife, so she can have them. I just think that when my toaster breaks this next time, I'm just going to try and see if I can live without it.

smile sometimes

We all have to try hard to smile, sometimes.
It's hard, but it's worth it, once you can get past the place
where you want to be someone else all of your life.
When you can just wake up
and feel ok with the skin given to you.
When the News Channel isn't a wet blanket
that covers your whole day.
When your wife is just as beautiful as the day you met her.
When everything smells fresh, like you've never been in NYC,
when beer tastes like beer
and not that foamy yellow corporate piss.
It's not much, but it's all I need sometimes to remind me that
life is good and very much worth living.

Loneliness has nothing to do with being by yourself,
sometimes.
Sometimes it has nothing to with whether or not people like
you, but rather if you like yourself.
Everyone thinks about dying from time to time, but these old
dreams of dying are making my bones feel sad, and are keeping
me from what I really want to do… be alive.
Breathe in, breathe out
Try your best.
Fail.
Repeat.
With every year that passes, I realize it's not about how many
things I can succeed at.

Rather, it's how I am able to deal with my failures.

We all have to try hard to smile sometimes.
Like a funeral parlor attendant who's tired of feeling sad.
Like Freddy Mercury's teeth.
Like telling your circumstances
that they do not dictate your well-being.
Rather, you control that way you feel
about your circumstances,
even when your circumstances are shit.
Even when you are at the end of your rope,
on the Fourth of July feeling very unpatriotic.
Even when your failures face you as giant failures.
You gotta try your best to smile, buddy.

a talk with my professional friend

The breeze sure is nice today as it blows on my skin. I light an organic mint scented candle on my front porch, as my neighbors argue over a parking spot. I empty the ashtray from last night, where we hung out on my front porch. Even though I don't smoke cigarettes anymore, a lot of my friends still do. Some of my friends are in their cubicles today typing and entering data, filling out reports, filling out spreadsheets, working on deadlines, earning the best living they can without a shovel in their hand, just trying to make ends meet with the gifts and talents that they let people see.

My one friend works on a floor that doesn't have any windows. No windows, no breeze, no sunlight. All day for about 40 hours a week, his only source of light is the fluorescent tubes in the ceiling above him, and the glow of the computer screen that is bleeding for his attention. On average, he sleeps about 8 hours every night for a total of 56 hours a week. So, in between the hours his eyes are closed while he is asleep and the 40 hours he is at his desk , makes just about 96 hours a week spent without seeing any natural light.

He leaves his house at 7:00 a.m. to walk to the bus stop. His bus gets him at 7:30, drops him off at 8:15. He gets a coffee and starts work at 9:00. He gets a half an hour (unpaid) lunch break from 12:30- 1:00 (second lunch shift). He works until 5:30 to get a full 8 hours so that he can keep his health care plan. After a day at the office, his bus gets him at 6:00, drops him off at 6:45, and he promptly walks home to let his dog out, who has now been franticly holding his bladder all day. It's now 7:00 p.m. After he takes the dog out to pee, takes him for a walk, and feeds him it's just about 8:00.

Tonight's dinner options consist of a peanut butter and jelly sandwich, canned ravioli, or leftover Chinese from the night before. He chooses the leftover Chinese. After dinner, he throws away his paper plate and plastic silverware. He decides if he is going to stay in and watch Netflix or go out and try and meet a girl. If he decides to go out, he only has about 2 hours to try and make a friend before he has to go back home, pack his lunch, shower, and go to bed so he can wake up for work the next day.

In order to upgrade his cable package to get all the hockey games during regular season, he works every other Saturday, a full 8-hour shift. The Saturdays in between that are usually spent at the laundromat, and cleaning his apartment just incase he ever does decide to bring a girl home. Sundays are the only day he really has free to do what he wants, but he usually is so exhausted from the grind of daily living he just kind of hangs out with his dog and drinks beer.

The last time we spoke, he seemed to be fine, didn't complain, didn't say too much of anything. He was excited that football season had started, but not because of football, but because that just meant hockey season is soon to follow. He told me he was ready for an adventure, he told me that he loved me. I told him that I was leaving town to travel to a far off land with mystery, danger, and excitement and I may not ever come back, and then I asked him if he wanted to join. He replied with "Dammit! I wish college offered a class on how to be a grownup and not hate yourself at the same time."

random thought pattern

You have got to question things...kids.
There are few things that are the way that they seem,
even good things.
Even the things that you work so hard to achieve,
once you capture them
they are rarely the way that you envisioned them.
Not every foot is going to fit into the same shoe.
College isn't for everyone.
Church isn't for everyone.
Cleaning your room isn't for everyone.
And punk rock certainly isn't for everyone.

Most hospitals aren't your friend.
They are a casino.
They are only there to take your money.
Think about the food they try to serve you
in the hospital cafeteria,
some microwaved pizza
or nasty breaded chicken finger and French fry meal.
If they really wanted you to get better,
they wouldn't try to just numb your pain
with the pills they are trying to sell you
with the insurance plans that only ever covers sickness
that you will never suffer from.

Don't buy new clothes; it's a giant waste of time.
Fashion is a fleeting roller coaster, going nowhere.

Adventure is the only thing worth giving your time to,
worth living for, worth dying for.
Safety is an illusion.
Eat great food from the dumpster.
Sew a patch on an old pair of slacks before you buy a new pair,
even if the patch doesn't match.
It's ok.

As long as you can learn to love what you have.
Learn to laugh at yourself; it's a great medicine.
Make love with your best friend every chance you can, it may
just save your life.
Try to go as many days as you can without being negative.
I've tried a million times; I can usually make it about a day and
a half.

I wonder if other people wonder
the same things that I wonder

I think I'm going to start wearing a wristwatch.

Nothing fancy, nothing flashy. Just a simple silver Timex piece with one of those metal elastic bands and maybe a light. I'm looking for a plain face, with a second hand. It doesn't have to be one of those ones you have to wind, but that may be nice.

It's not often that you see people my age wearing a wristwatch anymore. Everyone carries their time in their pocket . . . digitally, like a nervous tick. Like the train is always late. Like they're missing out on something. Like someone is going to say something bad about them on the Internet. Like they might miss out on making the first witty remark on some quasi-famous person's photo. Like they can't breathe without it. Like it's the only thing that brings them joy anymore. Like without it people may not think that they exist.

I think I'm going to start riding the train more often too. There are train tracks everywhere you look in this country, and I certainly haven't seen a fraction of them. I often sit and wonder where do they all go? And who still rides them? These old metal rails tell a story that I I'd like to hear.

The old men that are always at the coffee shop downtown have it pretty good. They sit and smoke cigarettes, roll dice, drinking wine and coffee all day, just laughing. None of them have a cell phone. They all wear a wristwatch. They look like the kind of people that would be waiting for a train somewhere, with a book in hand, just being present.

I bet they remember when things were still special. When

things could be new. When you had to go and find out for
yourself. When there was room to wonder. That would be nice.

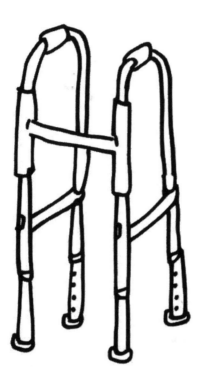

in my dreams I can fly

I've often wondered if I was the only 30 year old that still has dreams about flying. At least once a week I have this dream that I'm fbating through the hallways of Old Emerson Elementary School, floating above the heads of my classmates. It kind of works like swimming underwater, with the help of some magical fairy dust from Peter Pan. As long as you hold you're breath and think good thoughts, you can paddle through the air just as if you were swimming.

Now, I realize that most people my age are dreaming of buying a summer home, or buying a boat, or planning out some elaborate outdoor summer dream wedding with a folk band like The Avett Brothers playing traditional square dance tunes in a big old wooden barn. Maybe they have the same recurring dream every night about that raise or promotion, maybe even a dream that the Pittsburgh Pirates will win the World Series this year.

But not me, like clockwork once a week since before I can even remember keeping track, I have the same dream of me as a 10 year old in Bugle Boy clothing and dirty Converse All Stars, flying along the ceiling tiles in that old school building in West Mifflin, Pennsylvania laughing and giggling over the heads of my unsuspecting classmates. Sometimes in my dreams, I can remember laughing so hard that I almost pee my pants while floating through those hallways.

This was before I knew of politics, or puberty, before punk rock, or pornography, before the rape of religion, before the television took my tender heart. My mind, even in my dreams, was pure. It seemed to have an easy lightness to it that I can't describe all that well now. I can only recognize it when I feel it. Kind of like the feeling when you see a grand finale during a firework display kind of drunk on a blanket with some one you love, before they know that you love them. Like a first kiss, when you're unsure if they even really like you. Like seeing a handwritten letter or package in the mail, and you're unsure exactly what is inside of it, but so excited to find out. Kind of tingly. Kind of like how I feel now when I let out a good cry. Sometimes, in my dreams I can fly, and sometimes, even now as a 30 year old man, I wake up and try my best to hold my breath and take a swim in the air above me.

landfill

"So far, there has been a lot of dead ends," screamed the garbage man on his 50th birthday. "Almost everything you have ever touched, or will ever touch, will one day be put into a landfill. Things aren't made to last anymore, people grow so tired of things when they have lost their luster, when they've lost their shine. Every Pepsi bottle, every desk you ever sat on in school, every pen that has ran out of ink, every piece of homework. Most things they sell at Wal-Mart or the dollar store. Old kitchen appliances, old used cars, wedding dresses, used condoms, old hearing aids, old cell phones, and laptops. Every piece of clothing that has a tear in it that didn't get repaired is lying there moldy and rotting in the belly of some landfill.

"Do you know how many bags full of wrapping paper and boxes filled with Styrofoam are put on the curb the week after Christmas? How many copies of Guns and Roses' *Use Your Illusion I and II* cassette tapes are just lying in the ground forever, never to be used again? (Hallelujah.) How many pairs of plastic light up shoes or plastic Halloween costumes will be worn a handful of times then discarded, never to be thought of again?

"Every plastic fork and spoon in every cafeteria in every high school in America that was used once and just thrown away. Every Cleveland Browns jersey, empty detergent bottles, millions of disposable diapers, used tires, birthday decorations, balloons, streamers, 8-track players, Sega Saturns, Jaguar systems, and those millions of copies of the ET video game cartridge for Nintendo, that are buried somewhere in New Mexico, VHS tapes, snap bracelets, glow sticks, and plastic vampire teeth.

"And yet like clockwork, like lamb being led to the slaughter, you find yourself waiting in line with a plastic cart full of plastic shit the day after Thanksgiving year after year, using a plastic credit card to pay for a future plastic land fill.

"I wonder where my wife wants to go for dinner. I pray to God she says Red Lobster."

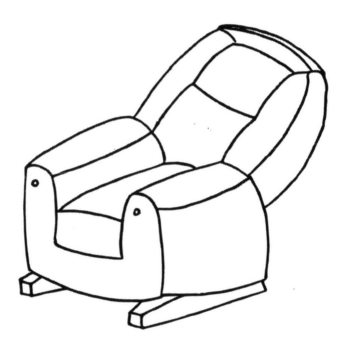

the peace in between everything else

How can I shut it off? How can I be free of this constant goddamn buzzing in my head? All day long from the moment I get my first sip of coffee, till the booze knocks me out at night, everyday from since before I can remember, it's been like this. Sometimes it starts off as a trickle, and only really starts to get bad when I feel lonely and bored somewhere around 2:00 p.m, but sometimes I'm up at 5 a.m. and the second I open my eyes it's like the flood gates have been lifted.

For example,
I just had 5000 new ideas
5000 brand new ideas
just now
just this very minute
all being processed
All at the same time.

What if these weeds would get pulled by a collective of people paid by the city to make it look nicer around here, like they can come by once a month with biodegradable garbage bags and clean this place up? Is there even a thing like that? Isn't that what our taxes are supposed to go towards? How can I get the shoes off the power lines? I think I want to create my own punk rock coloring book. Maybe I should call my dad. Fuck Tom Corbet! I hope my wife doesn't leave me. Am I too fat? I miss beer. I wish I had taken up skateboarding when I was a kid. I'm glad I'm not that guy. I wish I was someone else.

Is this hamburger gluten-free organic grass fed, or does it just say that on the menu to try and get you to spend a lot of money on a normal death burger?

I wonder if that girl knows she sounds like an idiot?
I'm glad I like the Beatles.
I wish I had hair like freewheeling Bob Dylan.
I had better sit down and write a song.
I feel stir crazy.
I need a walk.
Cabin fever, cabin fever, cabin fever, cabin fever.

I wish I had the money to do what I really want to do. I think I'm going to hop a train to Richmond. Will anyone really ever know me? Will I ever know myself? Have the lies I've told over and over become my reality? I'm just not going to pay my credit card bills anymore. Credit scores are a scam anyway. Taxes are a scam any way. Marriage is a scam anyway. Punk rock is a scam anyway. Money is a scam anyway.

Thank god for Pittsburgh, at least there is one place in the world that doesn't completely suck. I gotta get the hell out of this godforsaken town before I burst.

And then sometimes I can breathe, in between the floods and the trickles. And sometimes I have the strength to be a good friend, in between the wrecking balls crashing into the walls of my mind. And sometimes salvation comes when I can curl into a ball on my recliner, as my wife tells me she loves me just the way I am. And sometimes I can let myself believe her.

let go

When I go from here on to the next place
There is nothing I can take with me
No college degree
No amount of good looks
No collection of records
No fancy clothes
$150 sneakers
Or gold chains

When I go from here to the next place
There is no guarantee I'll be coming back
There is no guarantee that I know anybody there
There is no guarantee of much of anything
Other that it will be different than what we know right now
And sometimes that scares me

When I go from here to the next place
It will be too late to come back
And try to fix anything
Or take anything back
Or change someone's mind
About the emptiness we keep between us
About the walls we built to protect us from each other
To protect us from ourselves

And there are no short cuts here
There is nothing easy that is worth keeping
That is worth giving your time to
Or putting your name on

One Day those good looks are going to fade
And all the cleverness in the world won't mean a thing
New clothes will soon become old clothes
And there's no amount of records in the world
That can fill the empty storage spaces in your heart

Kindness is the only magic that exists in this world
It's the only thing that works
It's the only thing worth giving
It's the only thing that matters

Everything else is just waiting in a line somewhere
With a shopping cart full of rubbish that you hate to buy,
Like a funeral parlor yard sale
Like a ledger book of pluses and minuses
that you constantly check
Like a fever
like a parking meter
like not being able to let go

a commercial in the airport

Do you suffer from erectile dysfunction?
Do you have scars you wish you could get rid of?
Are you unhappy with the way you feel
about the way you look?

Great!!!

We have created a pill to help cure you of just about
everything. It's just expensive enough that you can afford it, but
not cheap enough for you to believe it doesn't work. Please
consult with your doctor or imaginary friend before using our
product.

This may not be for you if you are too old, too young, too
tall, too short, too fat, and too thin, if this is you, try your best
to get into our target demographic, the side effects are morbid
depression, self esteem issues, anorexia, head aches, heart aches,
heat attacks, stomach ulcers, explosive diarrhea, a bad attitude,
divorce, numbness of the hands and feet, numbness to reality,
you may see double, you may become more gullible, you may
develop an addiction to these pills, you may become addicted
to what other people think of you, you may become
brainwashed.

Do you hate your acne? Does your penis disappoint you?
Does your penis disappoint your partner? Then this pill may be
for you. Are you tired? These pills will keep you awake for days.
Do you find yourself listening to bad music? These pills will
sing you to sleep. Are you looking for an escape? These pills can

take you away from it all, your boring husband, bland sex life, stupid kids, poor career choices, these pills will wash your car, walk you dog, and be your very best friend, they will hug you if you are lonely.

Watch out for side effects, you may become dangerous when left alone. You may have regret. If this product doesn't work for you we have literally thousands of others for you to try to help you spend your money on things that will never make you feel better.

nothing

I am here
in the shower
with everything I came into this world with
and everything I will leave with.

The water is the most room temperature water you can have.
I turn the light off, it is dark.
I close my eyes
and get down on all fours like a dog.

The water hits my back and the back of my head.
The music is like a static that can put you to sleep.

I am relaxed,
there is no money,
there are no high school graduation nightmares,
and there is no job to go to.
There is just me,
my nakedness,
the water,
and the static music of the showerhead.

It feels like nothing; it feels like peace.

I breathe in deeply through my nose
and out through my mouth.
Thinking of only breathing.

No broken heart,
no suicide,
no television,
no politicians,
just nothing.

For the first time in my life,
I realize
that all I ever wanted
all I ever need
is nothing.
I am alive.

Derek Zanetti is a writer, musician, and artist from Pittsburgh, Pennsylvania. He lives in a house that he likes pretty good, that he bought with money he made from doing things that he loves doing. He loves to travel, and experience weird things with his friends and by himself. He loves to have huge potluck dinners, and loves to get letters in the mail. He gives great hugs, and can't think about one thing for too long. Other than that he's a pretty regular guy.

Made in the USA
San Bernardino, CA
10 January 2020